WHAT GROWN-UPS SAY & WHAT THEY REALLY MEAN

Also by Jim Eldridge

The Funniest Joke Book
The Wobbly Jelly Joke Book

By Jim and Duncan Eldridge

How to Handle Grown-Ups

WHAT GROWN-UPS SAY & WHAT THEY REALLY MEAN

Jim and Duncan Eldridge

Illustrated
by David Mostyn

Beaver Books

A Beaver Book
Published by Arrow Books Limited
62–5 Chandos Place, London, WC2N 4NW

An imprint of Century Hutchinson Ltd

London Melbourne Sydney Auckland
Johannesburg and agencies throughout the world

First published 1986

Set in Linoterm Century Schoolbook
by JH Graphics Limited, Reading, Berks

Made and printed in Great Britain
by Anchor Brendon Ltd
Tiptree, Essex

ISBN 0 09 942430 4

WHY YOU NEED THIS book

Grown-ups are liars. They lie to children, and they are convinced that children believe them.

For example, when a child asks a grown-up for something, or to go out somewhere, the adult won't say 'No' directly, even though he/she wants to. Instead the adult will say things like:

We'll talk about it later.

You'll have to ask your father/mother.

Wait and see.

I'll have to think about it.

I might.

Things are a bit difficult at the moment.

Are you sure it's what you really want/want to do?

When grown-ups want to avoid answering awkward questions, they say:

Now is not the time to discuss this.

I'm in the middle of reading/ironing/watching TV/scratching my nose.

Talk it over with your mother/father.

I didn't think you were interested in that.

We'll talk about it later.

I've got a sore throat, I can't talk.

Is it *really* important?

I'll have to think about that.

Why do they do this? Because they want to be thought of as 'nice' by everybody, including children. Well this is where we blow the gaff! Read this book and find out 'What Grown-Ups Say . . . (AND WHAT THEY REALLY MEAN!)'

POWER TO KIDS!

KIDS RULE OK!

OR?

At Home

Nobody cares about me. I cook, wash, and clean for the whole family, and I get nothing in return. Be a dear and wash up for me. After all, I know you care about me, you're different from the others. You don't want me to get ill, do you. *(Wash up and you'll get in my good books. If you don't I'll make you feel guilty.)*

What's this lying on the floor? *(I know jolly well what it is, but I want you to pick it up.)*

I want to have a serious talk with you. *(I'm going to tell you off.)*

It will do you good to have an early night tonight. *(I want you out of my way this evening.)*

You've had that shirt a long time. It's too small/too big for you. *(Don't wear that shirt, I don't like it.)*

Where were you this evening? *(I know where you were but I want to make you feel guilty for not telling me/coming home late.)*

How did you get on at school today, dear? *(I'm not the slightest bit interested, I'm only asking to be polite.)*

Your friend has a very interesting character. *(I don't like him/her.)*

Would you like to go on an adventure holiday? *(I'd really like to get you out of my way for a bit.)*

That TV programme you're watching doesn't look very interesting. *(Turn that telly off.)*

Nobody seems to take responsibility for the work in the kitchen. *(Do some housework.)*

How are you getting on with your homework? *(Hurry up and do your homework.)*

It's getting late. *(Go to bed.)*

That book you're reading doesn't seem very exciting/important for your education. *(I don't approve of that book, read something else.)*

You were late back from school today, dear. *(Why were you late back from school?)*

You're getting much too old for that childish little personal stereo of yours. *(I want that, give it to me.)*

If you were a girl/boy you wouldn't do that. *(I wish you were a girl/boy.)*

Your friend is quite nice really. *(Your friend is really horrible.)*

Nature hasn't looked too kindly on your friend, has it. *(Your friend is really ugly.)*

I suppose your friend's parents had difficulty in bringing him/her up. *(He/she is a right thug.)*

Don't forget, the doctor said because of your sore throat you mustn't use your voice too much.*(Shut up.)*

We've decided we aren't getting enough exercise, so we're going to do more walking, cycling etc., and we won't be needing the car any more. *(We're going to have to sell the car.)*

Your mother/father and I have decided we've been bringing you up wrongly by spoiling you too much. *(We're so poor we can't afford to treat you any more.)*

I think you ought to get a light part-time job like a paper round to give you practice at earning a living. *(I can't afford to give you pocket money any more.)*

I have a suspicion that you're allergic to chocolate. *(I can't afford to buy you any more sweets.)*

I heard on the news that computers/video games are bad for your health. They can cause headaches and backaches, and a survey showed that 80% of people who play video games suffer from stress. *(If you think I'm buying you a computer/video game you're mistaken!)*

You're much too old for a silly little bike like that, you need something more practical. *(I'm not buying you an expensive bike like that.)*

We're having some friends round for tea today, and I don't really think you'd find them very interesting, so I've arranged for you to go and see your friend. *(I'd feel embarrassed and ashamed if my friends saw your behaviour.)*

Those shoes you wear must be awfully bad for your feet, and as I care so much for your health I worry that they might cause you permanent damage. *(Don't wear those shoes, I feel embarrassed when people see you wearing them.)*

We've been thinking that it might not be a good idea to go on holiday abroad this year. With so many wars going on in foreign countries it's just too dangerous. *(We can't afford to go abroad this year.)*

I'm afraid Mummy/Daddy forgot to renew our passports, and they expired last month. We've sent away for them, but apparently the process takes months. *(We can't afford to go abroad this year.)*

It's time you learnt to do practical things, because there will come a time when I won't be around to do things for you. *(Wash up.)*

15

Oh dear, this cough of mine is getting worse. Go to the chemist and get me some cough medicine. Oh, and while you're there get.... *(Go and do the shopping.)*

Have you tidied your bedroom yet? *(I know you haven't tidied your bedroom. Go and do it.)*

This is for your own good. *(This isn't going to do you any good at all, but it eases my conscience to say it.)*

Do you really feel comfortable in that outfit? *(I'm not going out with you dressed like that!)*

Your bedroom is in an awful mess and I've got Auntie coming to stay and you wouldn't want her to get the wrong impression of you, would you? *(I'd feel ashamed if she saw your room. It would reflect badly on me as a parent.)*

Eat your dinner and you'll grow up big and strong like me. *(This doesn't mean a thing. I just want you to eat your dinner.)*

This soup has got lots of protein in it. *(This soup doesn't have any protein in it, but my mum/dad said it to me and made me eat it, so I'll say it to you.)*

I've been thinking that it would be nice to buy you something more expensive than usual for a present this year, and as your birthday is so near Christmas we could combine the two and give you one big present. *(I can't afford to buy you two separate presents this year.)*

It's much too hot to wear that jumper. *(Don't wear that jumper, you look silly in it.)*

I need to buy some food for us to live on, but I'm a little hard up, and if you want to eat you'd better lend me some money from your savings bank. *(I need some cash off you.)*

Your father/mother and I have decided it would be better for your sake if we lived apart. *(We're splitting up.)*

17

I've decided that you and daddy/mummy can manage quite well on your own and in many ways you'll be better off without me, so I shall be going away for a while. *(I'm off!)*

You should think yourself lucky, when I was your age I only got sixpence a week pocket money. *(I'm telling you this to make you feel you're getting a lot of money, but I'm hoping you won't twig that that was thirty years ago, and sixpence was a lot then.)*

You've been misbehaving so much lately I think I need to stop your pocket money until you've thought your behaviour over a bit. *(I need more money and this is as good an excuse as any to get it.)*

I do understand that each individual is entitled to his/her own point of view, but I think it's important that you respect and listen to mine. After all, you're only a child and you still aren't aware of all the facts. *(You're going to agree with me whether you like it or not.)*

Do you know there's a huge fair and carnival coming to our town this summer, and I know you'd just love to go. *(We're not going on holiday this year.)*

I don't think you should watch the television so much, it's bad for your eyes. *(I want to watch something else.)*

I wish you would model yourself on your friend. *(I much prefer him/her to you.)*

Dyeing your hair is very bad for it. It might even make it fall out. *(I feel embarrassed when you dye your hair.)*

Why don't you get the paperback version. After all, you might tear it, then all that money would be wasted. *(I'm not buying you a book that expensive!)*

Has your piano teacher made any comment on your progress? *(Stop making that dreadful row on that piano!)*

You were such a beautiful sweet darling when you were younger. (*You're getting really ugly.*)

Have you thought of taking an interest in classical music? (*I can't stand that awful rubbish you keep playing.*)

It would be unfair of me to put the responsibility of looking after it on your young shoulders. (*I wouldn't trust a clumsy twit like you with it.*)

That's all right, you can go out and have fun. I don't mind staying in on my own. (*You're not going out, because if you do I'll make you feel guilty.*)

It's surprising how you almost forget birthdays as you get older. (*It's my birthday next week. Don't forget it.*)

I do wish you wouldn't keep phoning your friends all the time. Everybody finds it very irritating with you hogging the phone constantly. (*Stop bumping up my phone bill with all your calls.*)

Your school report says you're not doing too well at English, so I think you should get some practice by writing to your friends instead of phoning them. (*I can't afford your being on the phone all the time.*)

I sometimes think I let you have things your own way too often. (*You're spoilt, and I'm going to be tough on you.*)

My, how you've grown! *(God, I'm getting old.)*

You *have* changed since I last saw you. *(Who the hell are you?)*

He certainly takes after his father. *(What an ugly child.)*

Do you want me to help you with your homework? *(I want to feel useful and impress you.)*

Ssssh, I'm thinking. *(I'm tired and I want to sleep.)*

I wish you'd be more like your father/mother. *(I can control your father/mother.)*

I don't know. *(I know but I'm not telling you.)*

I know but I'm not telling you. *(I don't know.)*

I know the answers to all those questions, but I think it's important that you find out for yourself. *(I haven't a clue.)*

When I was your age I respected adults. *(I did no such thing, but I wish you'd respect me.)*

I deliberately didn't give you any help with your Maths homework because I feel it is important that you work those sums out for yourself. *(I haven't a clue how to do them.)*

How long have you been wearing that shirt/
jumper/those trousers. *(Change them, they're
filthy.)*

Thank you, dear, it's just what I wanted. *(Ugh,
how can I get rid of it tactfully.)*

Did you make it yourself? *(What on earth is it?)*

When did you last wash your hands? *(Go and
wash your hands.)*

I sometimes wonder if I'm a bad influence on you.
(Tell me how wonderful I am.)

I'm concerned for your health. I think you're
watching far too much TV, so I'm moving it into
my room. *(I'm going to have the telly all to myself
from now on so I can watch what I want to.)*

I think those comics you read are having a bad
effect on your education. *(I'm not buying you any
more of those rubbishy comics.)*

What do you think of my new dress/suit/
hairstyle? *(Tell me how good I look.)*

When did you last wash/have a bath/shower? *(I
know when it was. I want you to wash/bath now.)*

How are you enjoying school? *(I can't think what
to talk about to children.)*

OUT AND ABOUT

Let's take the car into town, it's too dangerous to walk/cycle. *(I'm not fit enough to walk/cycle all that way.)*

I don't think that kind of garment suits you very well, and, besides, they'll be out of fashion in a couple of months. *(I can't afford to buy you expensive clothes like that.)*

Well personally I wouldn't choose that kind of thing, but you're entitled to your own opinion. However, I'm going to ask you to consider something else. *(I don't like that so you're not getting it.)*

We can't stop at the service station because it will make us late. *(I'm not having you wasting my money on video games/junk food.)*

Don't you think Uncle's new house is wonderful? *(I know it's a dump but say it's wonderful to be polite.)*

I do wish you'd eat a little more slowly. You'll get terrible indigestion if you don't, and also you're liable to spoil your food if you eat with your mouth open. *(Eat properly, you're embarrassing me.)*

I'm trying very hard to concentrate on driving and I find it very distracting when you keep mentioning things. *(Shut up.)*

It's just around the corner. *(It's at least another two miles.)*

This is educational. *(Stop fidgeting, I like museums/art galleries.)*

I loved museums when I was your age. *(I've got a bad memory.)*

Do you have to do that? *(Stop it, you're showing me up.)*

Over-eating is bad for you. *(I'm not buying you a big meal.)*

Let's not stop here, there might be a nicer place further on. *(We're not stopping anywhere if I can help it.)*

You don't have to eat it all if you can't finish it. *(Hurry up and finish your meal, I want some of it.)*

Do you want all your potatoes/meat/pudding? *(I want some.)*

You didn't have to come shopping with me. *(You did have to come shopping with me, and stop complaining.)*

Would you like to go on ahead? *(I'm not walking along with you looking like that.)*

I would like to get you a nice big stereo like that, but the problem is the walls are too thin and we'd have the neighbours complaining all the time. *(A big stereo would cost too much.)*

I don't think there is any point in me getting you nice clothes like that because you're still growing very fast and they wouldn't fit you after a month or two. *(Those clothes are too expensive.)*

As I've put myself out to bring you here today you might at least show some interest. *(I know this bores you but I wanted to come here.)*

I'm not going to support you in damaging your eyesight on those awful arcade games while we're here. *(I'm not giving you any money to play them with.)*

The speedo needle rattles between 40mph and 100mph and it drives me crazy, and I can't exactly crawl along the motorway doing less than 40, can I. *(I love driving fast.)*

I read in a magazine that a car becomes much more economical when driven over 70mph. *(I want to outrun the Ferrari coming up behind us.)*

It's much cheaper for us to travel by coach because our car isn't very economical. *(The car wouldn't start.)*

I thought it would be better for us to travel by train, you see so much more that way. *(Our car is a wreck, but I'm too proud to admit it.)*

I'm not travelling any faster because I consider it would be putting you in danger. *(I'm not going any faster because I haven't got the guts.)*

I'm not going any faster because this road is too bendy. *(My car won't go any faster.)*

That whining noise is just the wind. *(It's actually the engine, but I'm hoping you won't realize it.)*

I really don't think you'd like the food they cook in there. *(I can't afford to take you to a place like that.)*

I think we should wait until that film comes out on video, then we can see it in a far more relaxed atmosphere. *(I'm not taking you to see it.)*

I don't think you'd like this film I'm going to see. In fact it's not your sort of film at all so I've arranged for you to go and stay with a friend of yours for the evening. *(I want an evening at the pictures without you around.)*

Pop-corn/ice-cream/sweets is/are bad for you. *(I'm too mean to buy you any.)*

29

All the reviews I read of that film are pretty bad. *(I want to go and see another film, and as I'm paying that's the film we're going to see.)*

When I was young we made our own entertainments. *(I'm not giving you any money for video games.)*

We won't eat there, it looks very unhygienic and I'm sure the food will be terrible. *(It looks too expensive.)*

That popcorn you're eating is stopping me from hearing the film. I'll look after it and give it back to you after the film. *(I want to eat it.)*

We're not eating there, it doesn't look to me as if the food is very good value for money. *(It definitely looks too expensive.)*

I find it very irritating when you crunch popcorn all the way through a film. It spoils my enjoyment. *(I'm not buying you anything to eat.)*

He/she has been so looking forward to visiting his/her Gran/Aunt/Uncle, haven't you dear. *(Say 'Yes' and smile when you say it, or you'll be in big trouble when you get home.)*

Oh dear, I've run out of money. Lend me some until we get home. *(And that's the last you'll see of it.)*

I used to carry the heavy shopping for my mother. *(Carry the shopping.)*

While we're out I want you to be on your best behaviour so that people can see what a nice person you really are. *(Please don't show me up.)*

I'm only telling you for your own good. *(Your behaviour reflects on me as a parent.)*

Would you go and browse/look over there for a minute. I want to have a private word with your mother/father. *(We're going to have a row.)*

When I was your age I loved going for long walks. *(I want to go for a walk, no one else wants to come with me, so I'm going to make you accompany me. I'm your parent and you'll do as I tell you.)*

I think we ought to spend more time looking at our surroundings, instead of just rushing along. I suggest we sit down for a minute and admire the view. *(I'm worn out, but I'm too proud to admit it.)*

I don't think you appreciate the time, effort and money I've put into bringing you up. *(No, you can't have that radio/record/jacket/whatever.)*

School reports

GENERAL COMMENTS

Works well in class. *(Never in class.)*

A popular child. *(The school bully.)*

A good all-round worker. *(Useless at everything.)*

Shows great wit. *(Rude and insolent.)*

Shows an interest. *(But not in the school or any subjects.)*

Responds to a structured environment. *(Needs locking up.)*

I wish more pupils had his/her attitude to school *(and stayed away as often).*

We hope he/she will go far. *(We wish you would move to another district.)*

A lively child. *(A pain in the neck.)*

Lacks confidence in his/her own ability *(and quite rightly).*

A very individual achievement this year. *(Bottom of the class.)*

Needs lots of individual help. *(Are we sure this child is human?)*

A questioning mind. *(A troublemaker.)*

A leading figure in class discussions. *(Talks all the time.)*

Shows initiative. *(A thief.)*

Needs lots of attention. *(Ought to be kept tied up.)*

A valuable member of the class. (*Who is this child? I've never seen him/her before in my life.*)

Takes his/her opportunities. (*Takes anything if it isn't nailed down.*)

Has talent. (*But we haven't the faintest idea what in.*)

An example to the rest of the school. (*A bad example.*)

Tries hard. (*And keeps failing.*)

A forceful personality. (*A bully.*)

Very keen. (*Can't wait to get out of school when the bell goes.*)

A promising pupil. (*Always promising to work, never does.*)

A sensitive child. (*A vicious unspeakably nasty piece of work with psychopathic tendencies, liable to erupt into violence if things do not go his/her way*) or (*A wimp*).

Works hard. (*Achieves nothing.*)

With a little more effort he/she could achieve a good result. (*The lazy twit does absolutely nothing.*)

Achieved expected result in end of term exam. *(0 out of 100.)*

Has greatly improved this term. *(He/she couldn't have got any worse.)*

A good average member of the class. *(Don't know this child.)*

Has great potential. *(Never does any work.)*

He/she prefers outdoor activities. *(Plays truant.)*

An interesting personality. *(This child is dangerous!)*

Has trouble concentrating. *(Thick as a brick.)*

Could try harder. *(Never does anything.)*

His/her attention wanders easily. *(Ditto.)*

His/her achievement doesn't match his/her effort. *(Yes it does – nought effort, nought achievement.)*

ENGLISH

Spelling presents no problem. *(Because we can't understand his/her writing.)*

Shows an interest in books. *(Tears them up.)*

Is more proficient at reading than writing. *(Illiterate.)*

Writing presents some problems. *(Unable to take lid off pen without assistance.)*

A flair for creative writing. *(A liar.)*

Interested in literature. *(Steals books from library.)*

His/her best achievement is in oral work. *(Can't read, can't write, talks all the time.)*

Imaginative use of words. *(Foul-mouthed.)*

PHYSICS

Has an interesting future in electronics. *(Ought to be electrocuted.)*

Seems happy with this subject. *(Thick as a brick, but always smiling.)*

HISTORY

Has expressed an interest in history. *(Asked where he/she should have been yesterday.)*

Has stated that history is his/her favourite subject. *(Pity it's not shown in his/her work.)*

Has a good head for dates. *(Looks like a date.)*

Good exam result. *(Cheated.)*

RELIGION

Whenever I think of this child, I autometically relate him/her to this subject. *(Oh God!)*

MATHS

Has average ability for his/her group. *(The rest of the group are in the monkey cage at the zoo.)*

Advanced maths causes some problems. *(Has to take shoes off to count higher than 10.)*

Brain suited to geometry. *(A blockhead.)*

Has made some progress. *(Turns up for lessons now.)*

Has shown more interest in maths this year. *(Stayed awake in class more often.)*

GEOGRAPHY

Has problems with geography. *(Doesn't even know where he/she is half the time, let alone where the rest of the world is.)*

Seems comfortable with an atlas. *(Sleeps on it in lesson time.)*

GAMES

Useful in team games. *(Should be used as a goal post.)*

Sports are his/her favourite subject. *(Thick as a plank.)*

Has represented the school at both football and cricket. *(There are only eleven boys in the school.)*

CHEMISTRY

A keen interest in practical work. *(Blew up the laboratory on purpose.)*

LANGUAGES

Works hard at languages. *(But still having trouble with English.)*

Foreign languages will present no problems. *(Providing he/she never leaves the country.)*

WOODWORK

Has a great sympathy with the subject. *(Head like a plank of wood.)*

Has produced a great deal of work. *(Three bags of sawdust.)*

ART AND CRAFT

Made some progress with drawing. *(Has learnt to hold a pencil with the pointed end downwards.)*

Imaginative and unconventional approach. *(Draws on walls.)*

Has a basic knowledge of art. *(Able to get lids off paints.)*

An unusual artistic vision. *(Incompetent.)*

Immerses himself/herself in the subject. *(Gets covered in clay and paint.)*

RURAL STUDIES

Interested in plant life. *(Eats vegetables.)*

Has a future in Rural Studies. *(Would make a good plough.)*

At home in this subject. *(Brain like a cow.)*

MUSIC

Has a good ear. *(The rest of him/her is rotten.)*

Could have a future in music. *(Good at moving pianos.)*

An interesting ear for music. *(Tone deaf.)*

BIOLOGY

Some achievement in this subject. *(Knows what a person looks like.)*

COMPUTER STUDIES

Has a good grasp of the subject. *(Plays video games.)*

DOMESTIC SCIENCE

Achieved a great deal in cookery. *(Eats everything.)*

BOTANY

Is not really equal to the subject. *(Less intelligent than a plant.)*

POLITICAL SCIENCE

This subject is well suited to his/her talents. *(This child is devious, shifty, and not to be trusted.)*

TECHNICAL DRAWING

Produced some interesting work this year.
(Haven't the faintest idea what it was.)

I insist on absolute silence in my classroom. *(I prefer the sound of my own voice.)*

That child there, stop doing that or I shall report you! *(I can't report you because I don't know who you are.)*

This is Mr/Mrs Bloggs, who's kindly come to talk to you about his adventures as a carpet salesman in Birmingham/her life mending shoes in Bournemouth, which will be of great interest to you. *(I've fixed this so I can get two hours off.)*

You think you can get away with this, do you? *(You know you can get away with this.)*

I didn't behave that way when I was at school. *(I behaved just like that when I was at school.)*

Right, you, what's the answer? *(You obviously weren't paying attention and didn't hear the question, so I'm going to show you up in front of everybody.)*

No one in my class would do a thing like that. *(Of course someone in my class did that, but if I admit it it will reflect badly on me as a teacher.)*

Now although this is a Cup match, I want you to play a good clean game. *(Win at all costs, my reputation as a sports teacher depends on it.)*

Unless the culprit owns up I shall keep the whole class in after school. *(Please, please own up or I shall have to admit that I can't keep everyone in after all.)*

Unfortunately I shan't be in tomorrow. *(Hurrah, a break from you lot!)*

This exam is very important. *(This exam is meaningless, I just want to make you work hard.)*

If anyone else misbehaves I shall send for the Head. *(No I won't, because it will mean admitting I can't control a class.)*

When the whistle blows I want everyone standing ABSOLUTELY STILL. *(When the whistle blows just carry on as you always do.)*

Now when the visitors come round I want them to have a good impression of you, so let's see everyone hard at work. *(When the visitors come round I want them to have a good impression of me as a teacher.)*

I've never known such a badly-behaved class. *(Every class I take is as badly behaved.)*

I want you to achieve some good exam results. *(My promotion depends on it.)*

Team, I want you to make the school proud of you. *(Make the head teacher pleased with me for training you.)*

I will not tolerate this kind of behaviour any longer! *(I give up.)*

If you do that again you'll be in serious trouble. *(If you do that again I don't know what I'm going to do about it.)*

I won't tell you again. *(I will tell you again, and again, and again, and you probably won't take any notice of me.)*

I shall ignore that rude noise. Whoever did it is beneath contempt. *(I don't know who did it, and if I try to find out we'll be here for ever and then you'll get out of doing any work. Teaching you lot is like banging my head against a wall.)*

Right, just for that the whole class will sit up straight and remain in silence for the rest of the lesson. *(Great, I didn't have a lesson prepared anyway and now I can have a few minutes' peace.)*

I want you to check your work very carefully because I shall be going through it with a fine toothcomb – woe betide anyone if there are mistakes! *(I shan't even bother to read it, I'll just put a tick at the bottom of every page, and then a big tick at the end.)*

Because you've all worked so hard I'm going to let you off homework tonight. *(I don't feel like doing any marking.)*

I shall be in a meeting in the staff room this lunchtime and we don't want to be disturbed, so I don't want anyone knocking on the door asking for me. *(I'm going to have a sleep at lunchtime.)*

I do know who committed this offence, but I want that person to own up of their own accord. *(I haven't the faintest idea who did it.)*

On this school trip you will be representing the school, so I know you will all be on your best behaviour. *(I'm scared stiff you're all going to behave appallingly so I'm appealing to your better natures.)*

What we're going to do today in Maths/Science/Geography/etc. is revise and consolidate the work that we've done so far. *(I haven't planned a lesson for today.)*

It's about time you lot learnt some self-discipline, so today you're going to practise being quiet. *(I've got a hangover.)*

School dinners are balanced to give you proper nutrition. *(The school cook should be shot.)*

I don't want anyone else annoying the school caretaker. Be more considerate of him – he has a hard job to do. *(The school caretaker really runs this school, and he can get me sacked. Be more considerate of me.)*

When I was at school I was captivated by Shakespeare. *(I wasn't allowed to get out of reading him either, and like you lot I couldn't understand a word, but since I had to suffer him now you're going to.)*

Everyone here should be able to do these sums with ease. *(Especially me, because I've got the answers.)*

If you're not sure what to do, just ask me. *(And I will tell you to go away and work it out for yourself.)*

Well, this is the last day of the school year, and I would like to say how much I've enjoyed teaching you all. *(Unfortunately I can't. You lot are the worst rabble since Genghis Khan and his mob.)*

I've worked very hard to improve your standard of education, but . . . *(I've done nothing, you've done nothing. Was it worth us even turning up?)*

Do you think I enjoy telling you off all the time? *(I do, actually. It gives me a feeling of power.)*

how to deliberEATely

mISUNDERSTAND

ADULTs double-talk

AN ADULT

When an adult asks you 'What's that on the floor?' (meaning 'Pick that up'), be very 'helpful' and answer their question: 'It looks like a piece of paper – or it could be a piece of fluff. Hang on, it's a drop of porridge. . . . No, no, it's . . . I'm not really sure. Have you got any ideas?'

By this time the adult in question will be having a nervous breakdown. Try this trick a few times and you will soon have your adults well trained: they will pick the thing up for themselves, rather than go through it all. The alternative is for them to order you to pick the thing up – and if they do you can counter-attack with, 'But I didn't drop it. . . .' This can develop into an investigation of who did drop it, and by the time they've discovered that it really was you after all, the dog will have eaten whatever it was.

To explain what I mean in greater detail, here are some examples from my infamous 'Diary of X', showing how I dealt with grown-ups who tried it on me. . . .

What grown-ups say

and what they really

MEAN

is Proud to present

THE

DIARY OF

X

Friday 13th

A suitable date for today's entry. A truly terrible day. Today I am being turned out of my home by my unfeeling parents. Ah well, it had to happen. I suppose it must be hard for them to live with a genius like me. I fought against it, of course, but for once I lost.

It came like a bombshell yesterday at breakfast. I'd just started on my second helping of cornflakes (the last lot in the packet, but I'd persuaded Dad that he was getting fat), when Dad said, 'Your mother and I think you're looking under the weather, and that a couple of weeks by the sea would do you good.'

Well, I was delighted. All those hints I'd dropped about underprivileged children who never go on holiday had finally worked. Then came the bombshell: 'So we've arranged with your Uncle Steve and your Auntie Sheila for you to stay with them for the next two weeks.'

I nearly choked on my cornflakes. Uncle Steve and Auntie Sheila are two of the most mindless people ever invented. They're an ageing hippie couple who live on a marsh somewhere on the East Coast, where the land is so flat they have to tie the grass down to stop it blowing away.

It is a truly terrible part of the universe, and Uncle Steve and Auntie Sheila are two really zapped-out idiots, who wander round simpering

at people and going 'Peace and love'. If anything upsets them they say things like, 'Man, this is too heavy for me,' and 'We should communicate with the universe more.' In short, they are wimps calculated to drive any sane person to banging his/her head against a wall.

They don't believe in video games, they don't believe in pop radio, and they only have a television for Uncle Steve's Open University Course.

'Uncle Steve and Auntie Sheila?' I croaked, aghast.

'We thought you'd be pleased,' said Dad.

'And it will do you good,' said Mum.

At first I was too stunned even to object – how could they do this to me? And then I started:

1. The damp marsh climate would bring on rheumatism, asthma, flu, pneumonia, the plague.
2. Being miles from anywhere would lead me to become a lost and lonely child.
3. Uncle Steve and Auntie Sheila weren't near the sea. No one on that part of the East Coast was near the sea because there were mud-flats a hundred miles wide between the marshes and the sea. I would disappear in the mud-flats and never be seen again.
4. Uncle Steve and Auntie Sheila were peculiar and their hippie life-style would lead me astray.
5. I wanted to stay near the parents I loved (Sob).

Etc. etc. etc. and so on. All to no avail.

In short, what Dad and Mum were saying when they said 'We think you're under the weather and that a couple of weeks by the sea will do you good,' was: 'We can stand you no longer. If we could we would tie a heavy weight around your neck and drop you in the canal, but failing that we are going to inflict you on Steve and Sheila. We will then be free of you for two weeks, and maybe suffering their wimp-like life-style will make you appreciate us more, and toe the line when you get back.'

All was lost. It was with a heavy heart that I went down to the video arcade. It was no consolation playing on Dad and Mum's feelings of guilt, and conning them both (separately) out of a pound to play the games – or even conning the arcade manager into letting me have a free game after I'd 'lost' a non-existent coin in the slot.

I was doomed to go to Steve and Sheila's.

Saturday 14th

Today I was dumped on the lunatic fringe of the family (Steve is Dad's brother).

All my last-minute efforts to get a reprieve were to no avail: racking coughs, stomach pains, suspected leprosy, dizziness, home-sickness, travel-sickness, all came to nothing. Even my appeal to my mother as I handed her my old bus pass ('Take this. If anything should happen to me while I'm away, look at it and remember me') had no effect. How hard-hearted they are. (*Mental memo:* while I'm away I shall make an anonymous phone call to the police and tell them my disappearance is due to being murdered, and my body is buried in my dad's favourite flower-bed. When his begonias are dug up by hundreds of coppers he'll regret sending me away.)

Steve and Sheila met me at the station with their usual wimp-like niceties: 'Hey, how wonderful to see you again. It's going to be fun having you around.' (*Translation:* 'We didn't want you to come here, but we couldn't get out of it because we owe your parents too many favours.')

I smiled politely and let them show me the view as they drove me back to their hovel in the middle of the marsh: 'Look at the scenery. You can see for miles.' (*Translation:* 'This is the flattest, most boring piece of country in the world but it's cheap because no one in their right mind would want to live here.')

When we arrived back at their place – 'It's not very plush but it's our kind of house.' (*Translation:* It's a dump because we can't be bothered to do anything to it, like sweep up) – Sheila suggested that I must be tired after my long journey, and maybe I'd like to have an early night. (*Translation:* 'Let's get this kid out of our way at the earliest opportunity.')

I countered by saying that I had been so looking forward to seeing them again that I would rather spend my first evening in their company. The sight of their faces falling was a joy to my heart.

Our first evening was the ultimate in boredom: they read books and listened to Radio 3. This was too much for me and I decided to give them the First Round, and went to bed.

A plan is forming in my brain. These two weeks could be fun after all. I am going to take on Uncle Steve and Aunt Sheila and stir them up. They have always been so laid-back and wimplike, pretending to be so 'caring', that I'm determined to make them crack and give vent to their real feelings.

I am going to force them to stop lying when they say things, and get them to say what they really mean.

Yes, these two weeks could be fun.

Sunday 15th
Into the attack today. Got off to a flying start when Uncle Steve was showing me some of his wood carvings.

'Of course,' he said with lots of false modesty, 'they're not really very good.'

It was his way of saying they *were* very good, and getting me to agree, and say, 'Oh, really, they're wonderful', or some such guff. Instead I nodded sympathetically and said, 'Not to worry, I'm sure lots of other people find wood carving just as difficult as you do.'

This threw him, so he added rather pointedly: 'Of course, Sheila thinks they're very good and says I ought to exhibit them.'

I just smiled sympathetically and said nothing. That rattled him.

Monday 16th
Shopping with Aunt Sheila today.

Standing in the shop, she said, 'I'll carry this big heavy shopping bag back to the car.'

(*Translation:* 'This shopping is too heavy for me, so would you carry it? I'd ask you directly, but I don't want to be thought of as a bossy adult.')

I was supposed to reply, 'No no, Auntie, *I'll* carry that one.' Instead I said, 'Very well, Auntie, if you'd prefer it that way,' picked up the little bag, and carried that back to the car.

The big bag was so heavy Aunt Sheila's put her back out. That'll teach her.

Tuesday 17th
Think I'm getting through to Uncle and Auntie. Caught them glaring at me today, though they broke into happy smiles when they saw me looking at them. They also came up with, 'We thought it would be nice for you to get the feel of

the country around here without us hanging around you today.' *(Translation:* 'Keep out of our sight today.') I countered with: 'No no, my pleasure is in your company.' That wiped the smiles from their faces.

Wednesday 18th
The swines! They've made a really vicious move against me: they've got rid of the telly! They said, 'We thought while you were here we'd lock away the television. After all, it gets in the way of conversation, and you said you preferred the pleasure of our company. As you feel that way, we thought it was the least we could do.' *(Translation:* 'We've hidden the telly. *That'll* force you to leave.') The swines.

Thursday 19th
Found the telly today. The crafty pair had hidden it in their bedroom, under a cloth.

Used ruse to get it back into the living room: I told them that the late film on the telly was of a book we were doing at school, and our English teacher had told us all to watch it. I asked if I could join them in their bedroom for this special occasion and watch the film on the telly. As I expected, under the threat of me invading their private room, the telly reappeared.

Rather than take a chance on it being removed again, I put superglue on the television table, so it stuck when they put it down.

A close shave. Do not underestimate these people.

Friday 20th

A classic line from Aunt Sheila today: 'We thought you might be feeling guilty about not helping around the house, so we've made a list of jobs for you, to make you feel more comfortable.' (*Translation:* 'We're sick of seeing you do nothing but laze around, so we're going to make you work.')

This was easily dealt with by doing the jobs wrong (broke the axe while chopping wood; broke two plates and a cup while washing up; fed the dog too much dog food, with the result it was sick all over the carpet.)

All in all, a successful day.

Saturday 21st

Uncle Steve and Aunt Sheila's patience definitely wearing thin. Their smiles are now starting to look a little stretched, and they're starting to snarl a bit. Today Uncle Steve's 'caring' manner slipped. It started with him giving me a friendly: 'I bet you can't run down to the post box and back in three minutes.' (*Translation:* 'Post this letter for me.')

I said: 'You're right, I can't. I'm no good at athletics.'

He tried again with: 'Haven't you got a letter to post to your parents?' I said: 'No, they said there was no need to write to them.'

At this his cool slipped and he snapped: 'Take this letter to the post box, you crafty little. . . .' I immediately expressed 'surprise', and said

sadly, 'I'm sorry, Uncle Steve, I didn't realize you wanted me to run an errand for you, or I would have offered with pleasure.'

This caused a right royal row. As I was leaving the house with the letter, I could hear Aunt Sheila telling Uncle Steve off for being so unkind and raising his voice to me; and Uncle Steve telling her if she thought I was really so innocent then she had the brain of a paralyzed chicken.

Another one to me.

Sunday 22nd
Day off. Stayed in bed.

Monday 23rd
The swines got me again!

This morning they said, 'We're going to a talk on yak acupuncture in Tibet this afternoon. We know you'll be bored by it and you'd prefer to have the afternoon on your own.' This was such an unsubtle way of saying, 'We're going off on our own to get away from you this afternoon,' that I nearly laughed out loud. However, keeping to my discipline of losing no chance to call their bluff, I said: 'Oh no, I'd love to go with you. Yak acupuncture fascinates me.'

So I went with them . . . and they really did take me to a three-hour talk on yak acupuncture. The swines! Three hours of sitting in a draughty hall watching some bloke show slides of pins sticking in a yak's foot.

They'll pay for this!

Tuesday 24th

Tonight Steve and Sheila threw a dinner party.

Actually it wasn't the *party* that should have been thrown, it was the food. Seaweed fritters. Burgers made out of grass.

The place was full of people with head-bands on, being patronizing to me and saying things like, 'I really relate to kids.' (*Translation:* 'I have a mental age of four'); 'What are you going to do when you leave school?' (*Translation:* 'I haven't the faintest idea what to talk to children about, so I'll lead the conversation towards talking about adult work'); and 'Childhood is such a precious time of life.' (*Translation:* 'I'm glad I'm not a kid any more.')

There were also those who wanted to lead me into saying nice things above Steve and Sheila: ('They're such a nice couple, aren't they'), and those who wanted me to slag them off by contradicting the very same phrase. (*Translation:* 'They're not really as nice as they pretend to be, are they? Tell me something that will show how rotten they really are.')

I had one moment of fun with one nasty 'artist' twit, who said in a confidential way: 'Of course, your Uncle tries hard with his carvings, but what a pity about his talent' (*translation:* 'Let's be rotten about your Uncle together'), to which I said: 'That's funny, that's exactly what he said about you.'

That put the bloke out, but after that the party got boring, so I threw up over a woman and went to bed.

Wednesday 25th
Chaos today.

Last night's 'do' put a few cats among a few pigeons. Apparently the artist twit I had a go at last night is Aunt Sheila's art teacher at evening class, and she think's he's so wonderful and the sun shines out of his ears. So, when she heard from him what I told him Steve had said about his paintings, she was livid. I woke up this morning to hear her yelling at Steve, saying he was jealous of Roland (this artist twit) because he had 'real talent'. This got up Uncle Steve's nose and he said if she thought Roland's paintings showed any signs of talent then she either needed glasses or a brain transplant.

He then said it was a pity I'd been sick over

73

Roland's wife (so that's who the woman was) instead of over one of Roland's paintings as it would have improved it.

Decided it was time to get in on the action, so I hurried downstairs and strolled into the kitchen with a cheery 'Hello'. They both shut up, so I stirred things up by being 'apologetic', and said, 'I'm sorry I was sick last night. I tried to get to the toilet in time. I hope that woman and her husband weren't upset; they seemed a nice couple.'

This brought a strangled noise from Steve, and Sheila said, 'You'll have to excuse your Uncle Steve, he's feeling a little under the weather this morning.' (*Translation:* 'We've had a row and I'm going to rub his nose in it.')

This being too good an opportunity to miss, I threw in an 'innocent': 'Is that man a good artist? He seemed to know a lot about painting.'

That did it. Steve burst out with; 'That man wouldn't know good art if you banged him over the head with it.'

Sheila came in sharply with, 'I really don't think our nephew is interested in your views on someone else's talent.' (*Translation:* 'Shut up, Steve'), so I came in with: 'Oh, but I am.'

At this Steve opened his mouth to really lay into Roland, but Sheila went all tight-lipped and grim-faced and cut in with, 'I really think we all ought to get on. There's a lot to do in the house today.' (*Translation:* 'Steve, shut up. You and I will argue about this in private later.')

Steve shut up, but the look on his face said an awful lot.

74

Thursday 26th

Day off today. Steve and Sheila not talking.

Went into town on my own for the afternoon. Annoyed a bloke in a café by making a cup of coffee last an hour. He kept coming up and saying, 'Would you like anything else?' (*Translation:* 'Order something or get out'.) I smiled politely and said 'No' every time.

When I finally left and paid, he said, 'Service isn't included.' (*Translation:* 'I want a tip'), to which I smiled politely and said, 'Quite right too. Give the customer a choice,' and just walked out.

Friday 27th

Found out yesterday afternoon Sheila went to visit Roland ('to make sure his wife wasn't upset over Tuesday night').

This led to an almighty row, with Steve accusing Sheila of fancying Roland. Great stuff. Plates and saucepans flying all over the place.

Steve finally said, 'I think we ought to leave this until we've both cooled down.' (*Translation:* 'I'm losing, so let's call a truce.').

I said (helpfully), 'Is there anything I can do?', to which Steve said, 'Yes. Go and drown yourself.'

I turned to Sheila appealingly and said, 'Auntie Sheila, do you think I deserved that?' She said, 'Yes.' So, another successful project: two people made honest.

Saturday 28th

Well, all good things come to an end. Today I went home. Uncle Steve and Aunt Sheila didn't

say, 'It was wonderful having you here', so I guess they're cured.

My parents, on the other hand, said, 'It's good to have you back', which I know to be a lie, meaning 'Oh no, not you again'.

I can see I'll have to take these people in hand.

Well, there you have it. By now you should be able to understand Grown-upese (a language on its own). If adults still baffle you sometimes when what they say is obviously untrue – or just doesn't make any sense – then check again with this book for a translation.

If their contradictory words still have you wondering, then it could be that your particular grown-up is more cunning, more cowardly, more hypocritical, or simply more stupid, than most.

In which case, why not keep a log yourself of things *your* grown-ups say, and what they really mean:

My parents say ....

    but mean ....

My teacher says ....

    but means ....

My gran says ....

    but means ....

Politicians say ....

    but mean ....

All the best, and don't let them beat you!

HOW TO HANDLE GROWN-UPS

Jim and Duncan Eldridge

The hardest questions adults ever ask are 'Why?' and 'Why not?' With Jim and Duncan Eldridge's HOW TO HANDLE GROWN-UPS you will always have an answer . . .

★ Why haven't you done the washing up?
   There was a spider in the sink and I didn't want to kill it.

★ Why were you late for school?
   I found out that signals from space satellites have interfered with my digital alarm clock, and it went off an hour late.

★ Who broke my favourite bowl?
   It was like that when I came in.

101 excuses and reasons for getting out of everything.